LET'S COLC

THE WORLD

Coloring book

For kids age 4-6

By

ANNE LEDDES

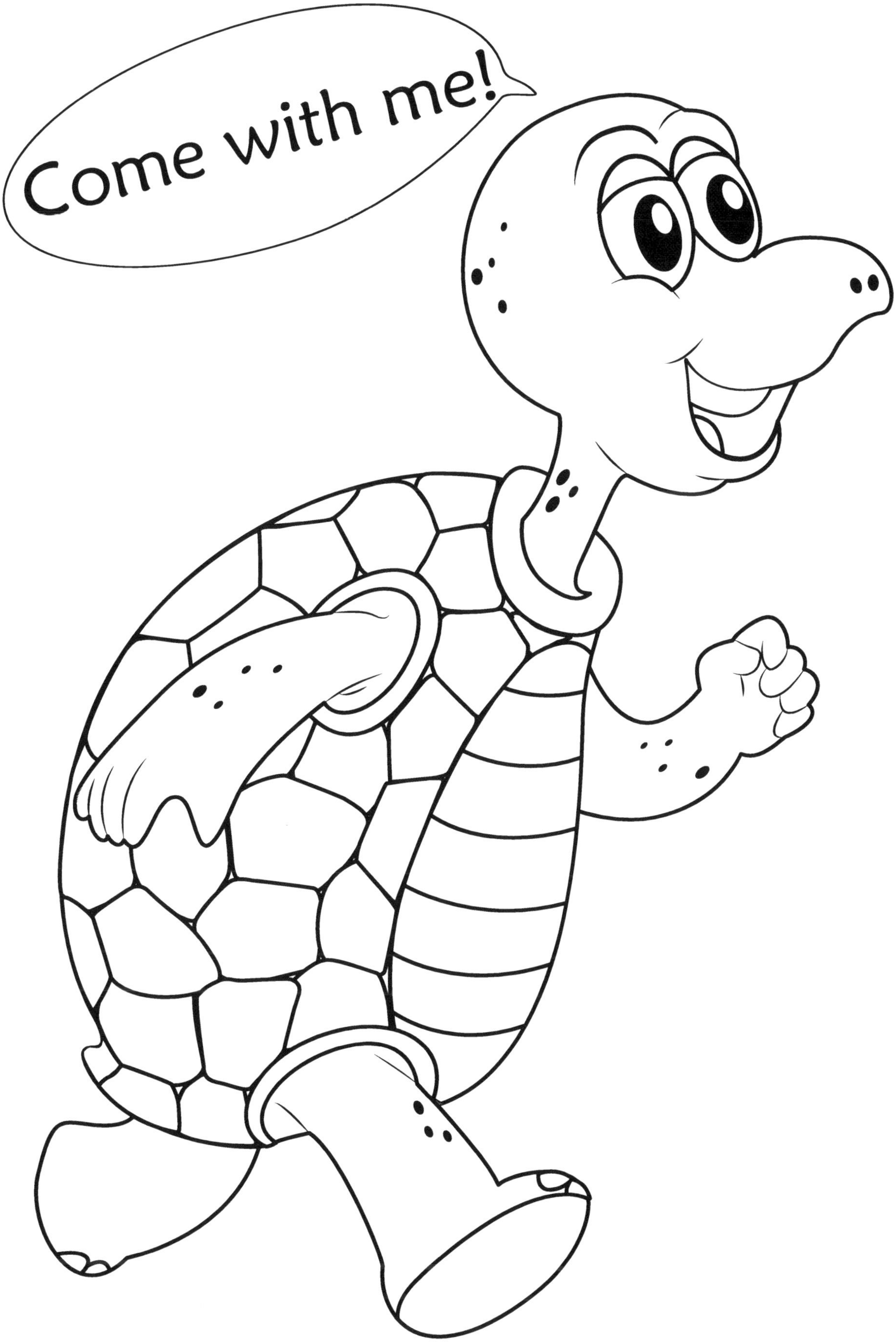
Come with me!

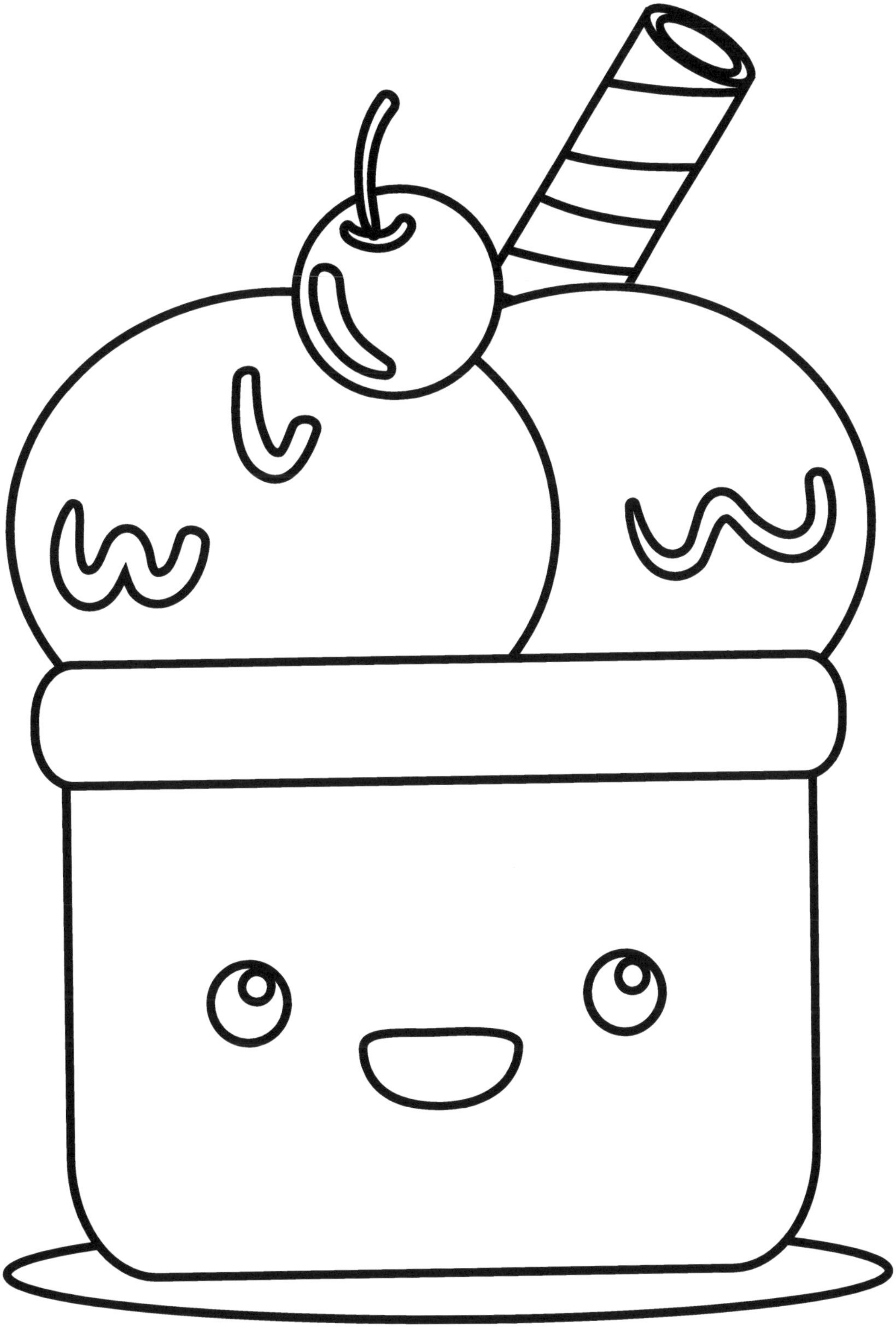

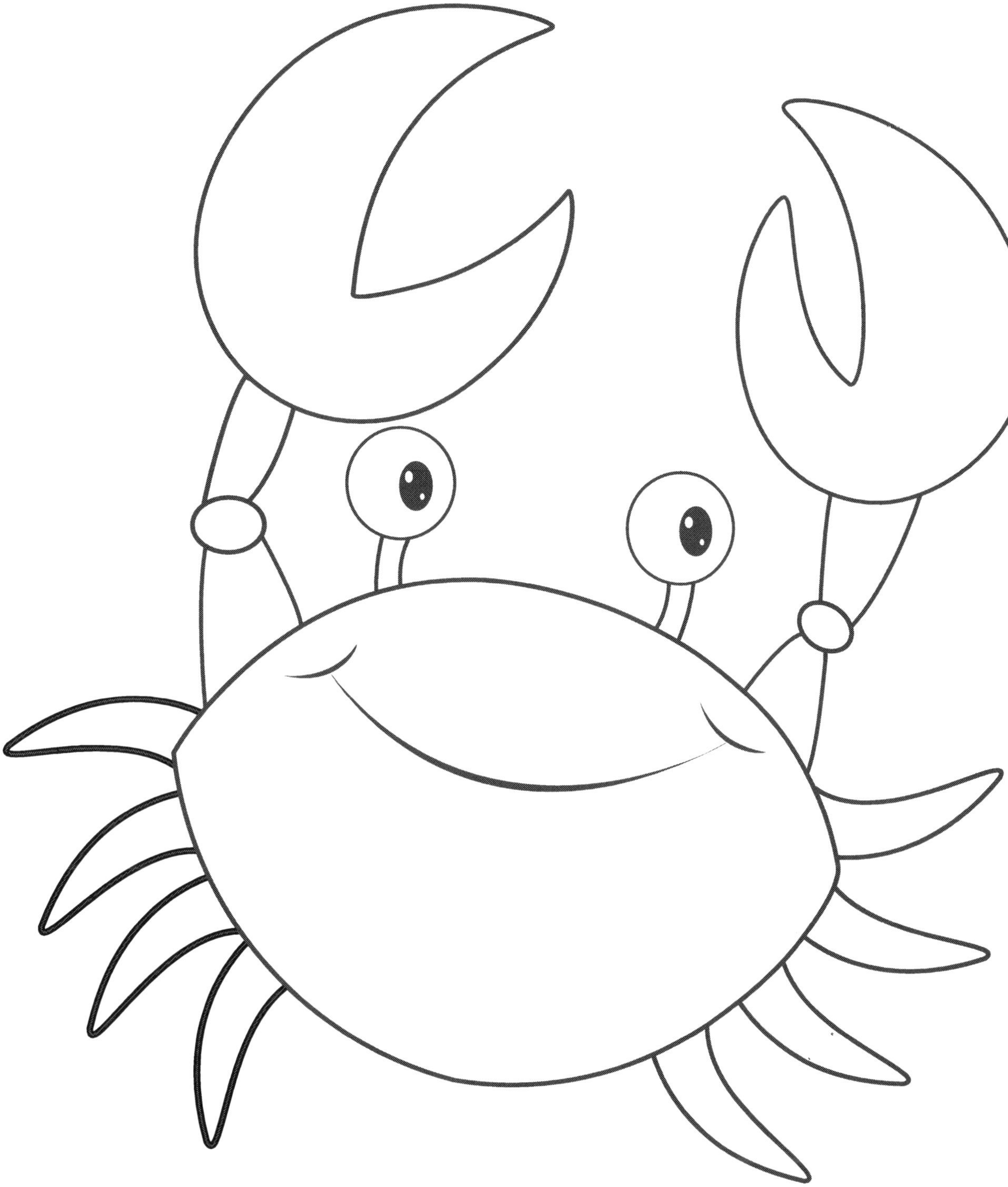

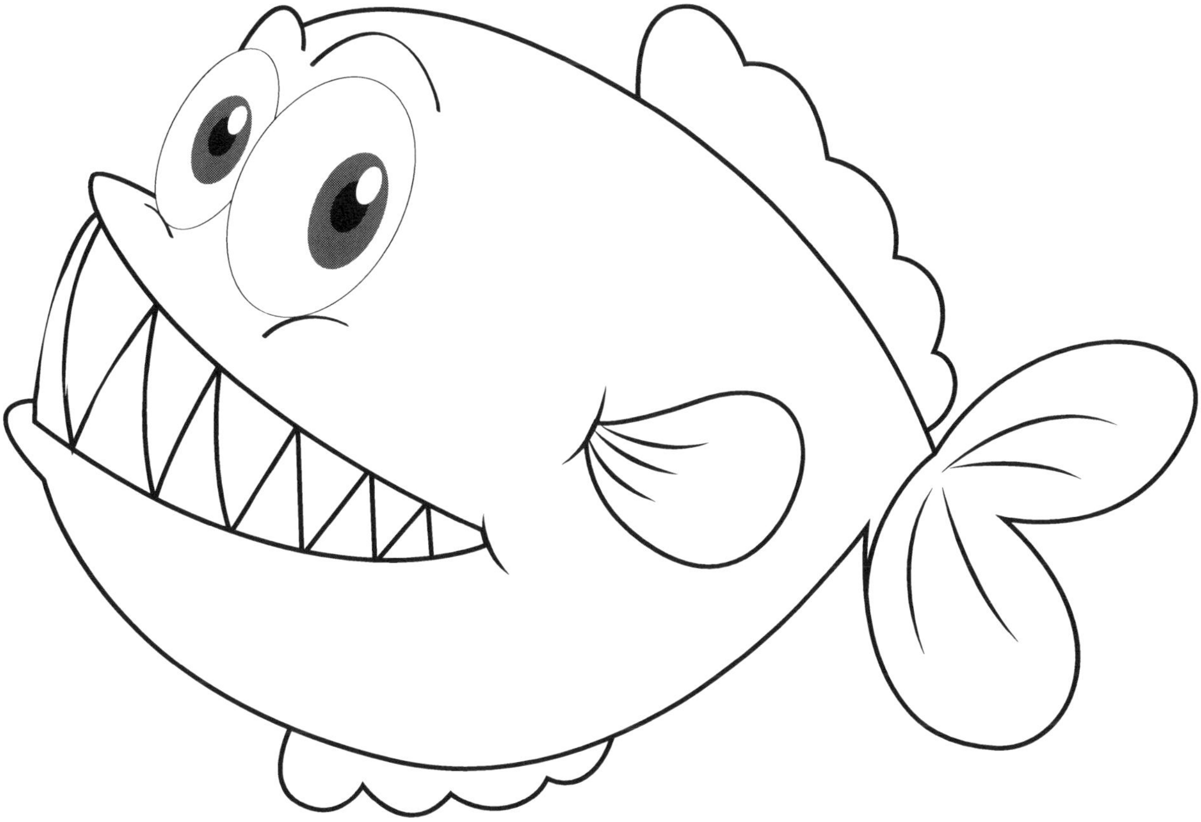

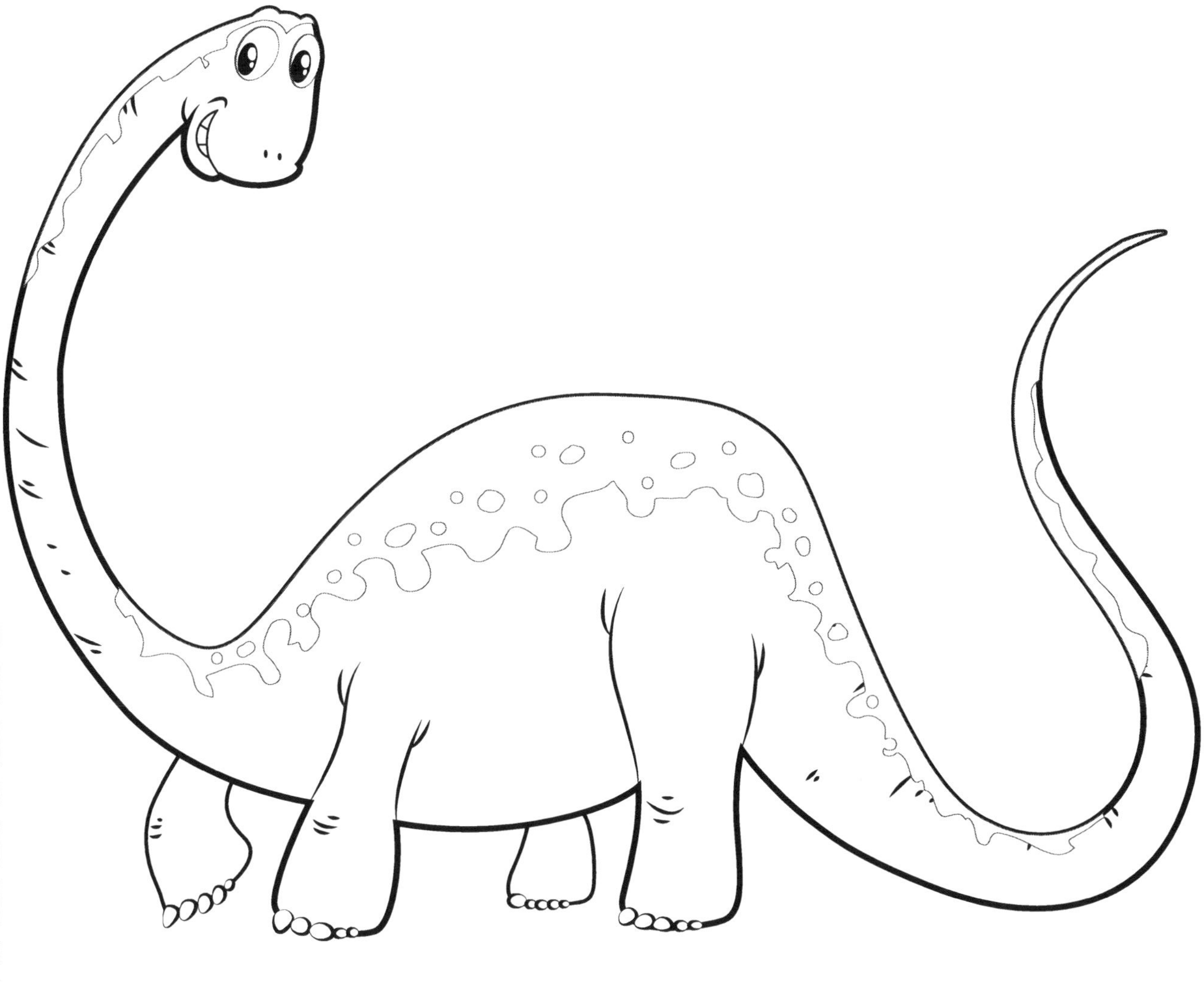

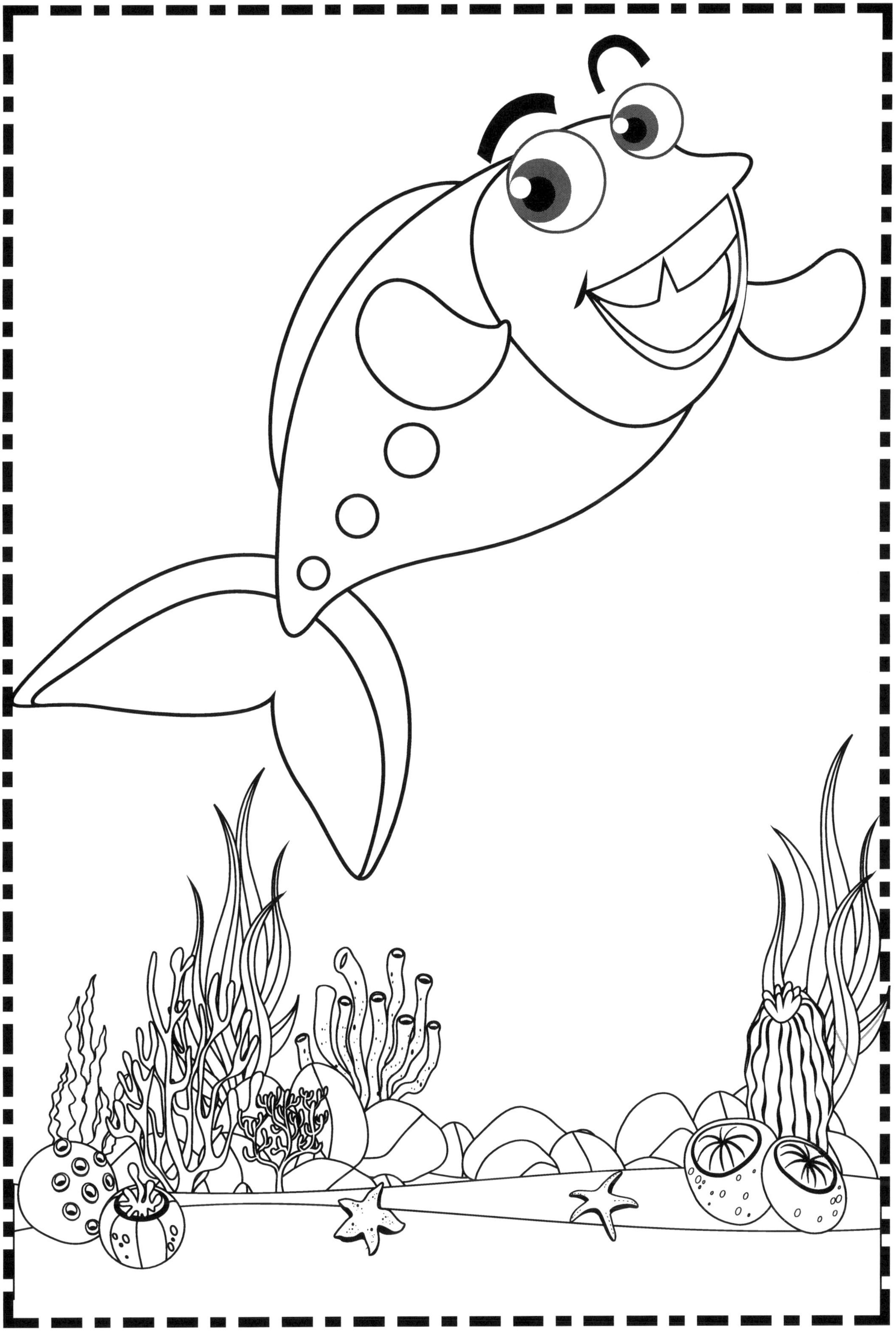

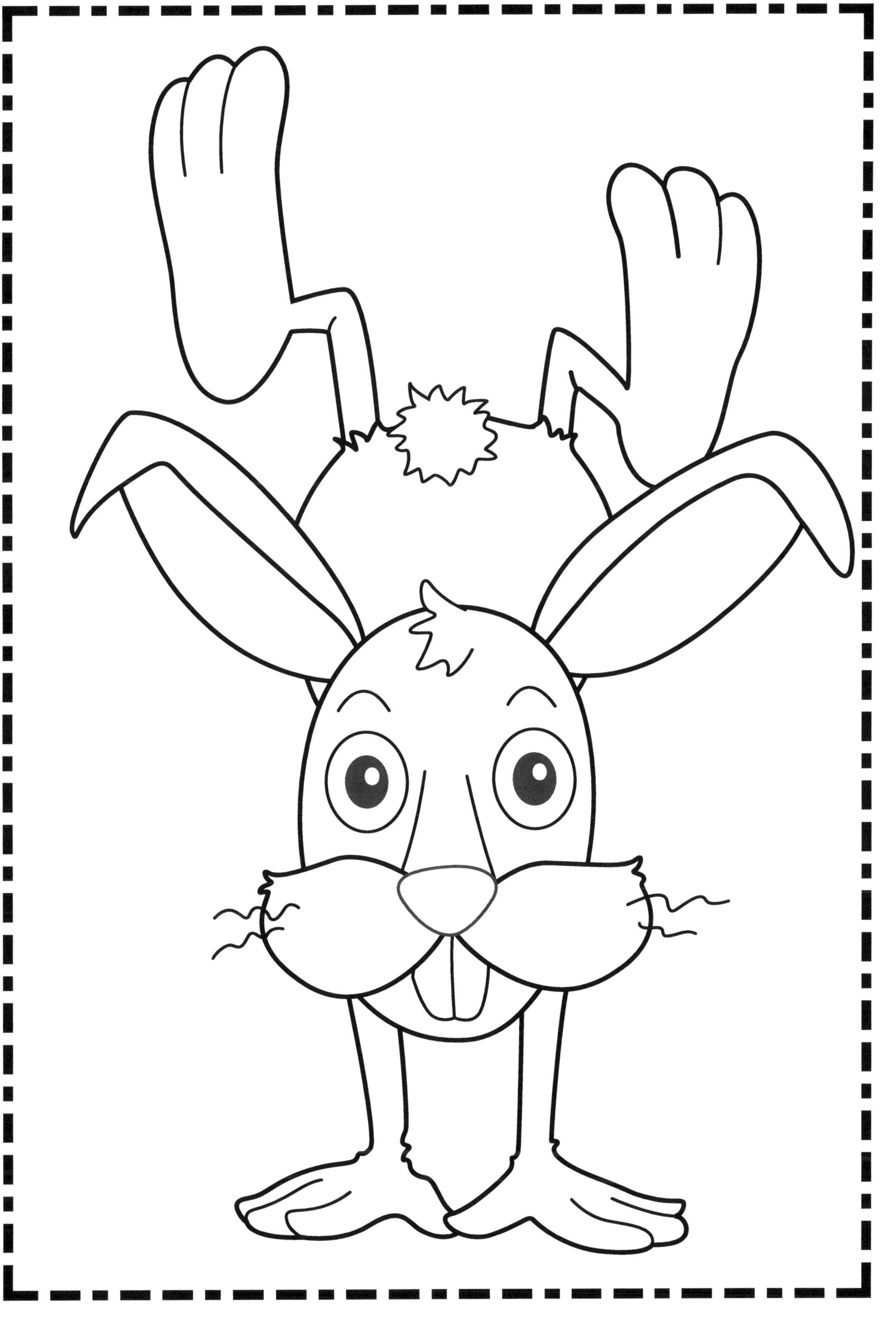

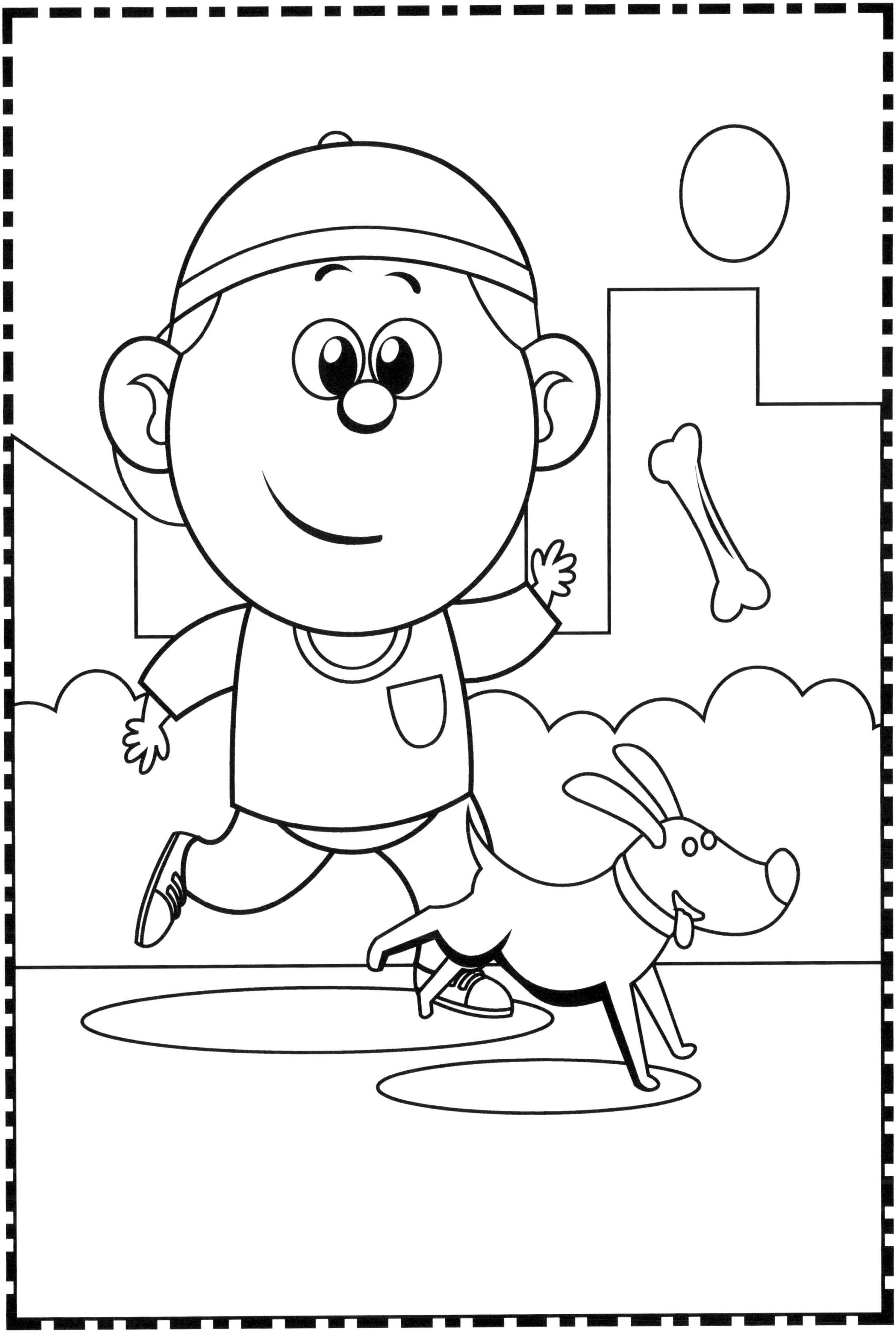

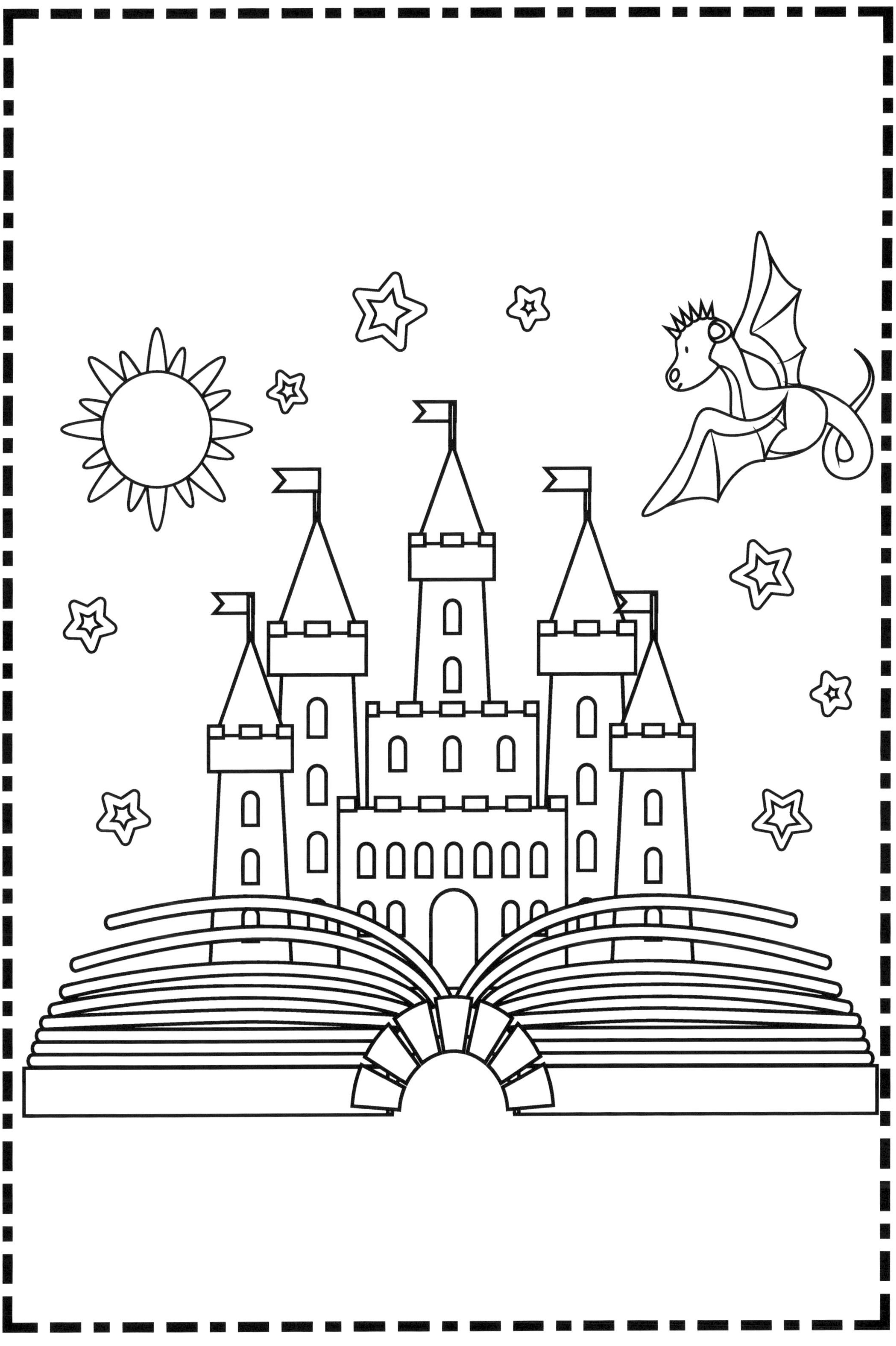

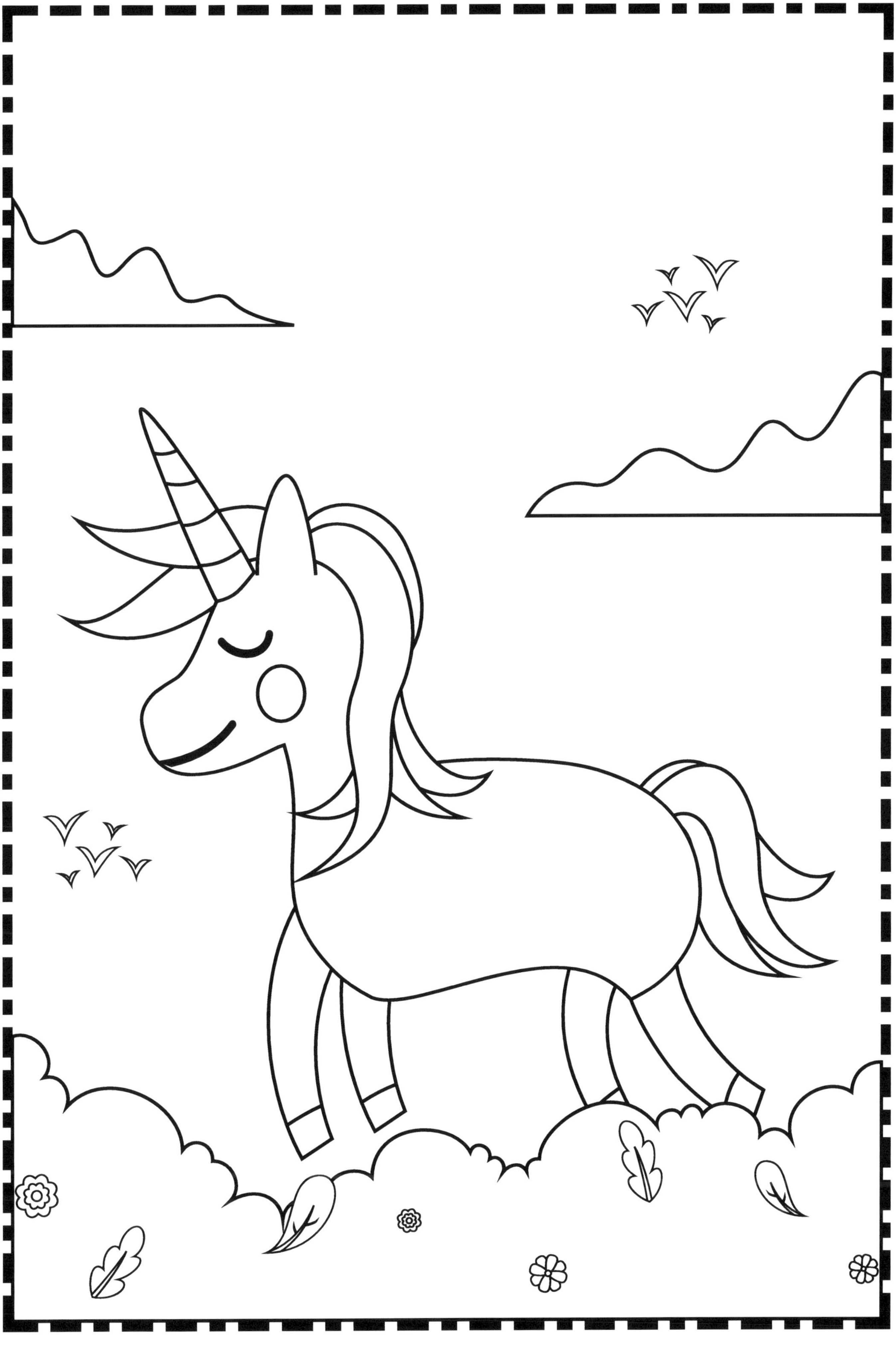

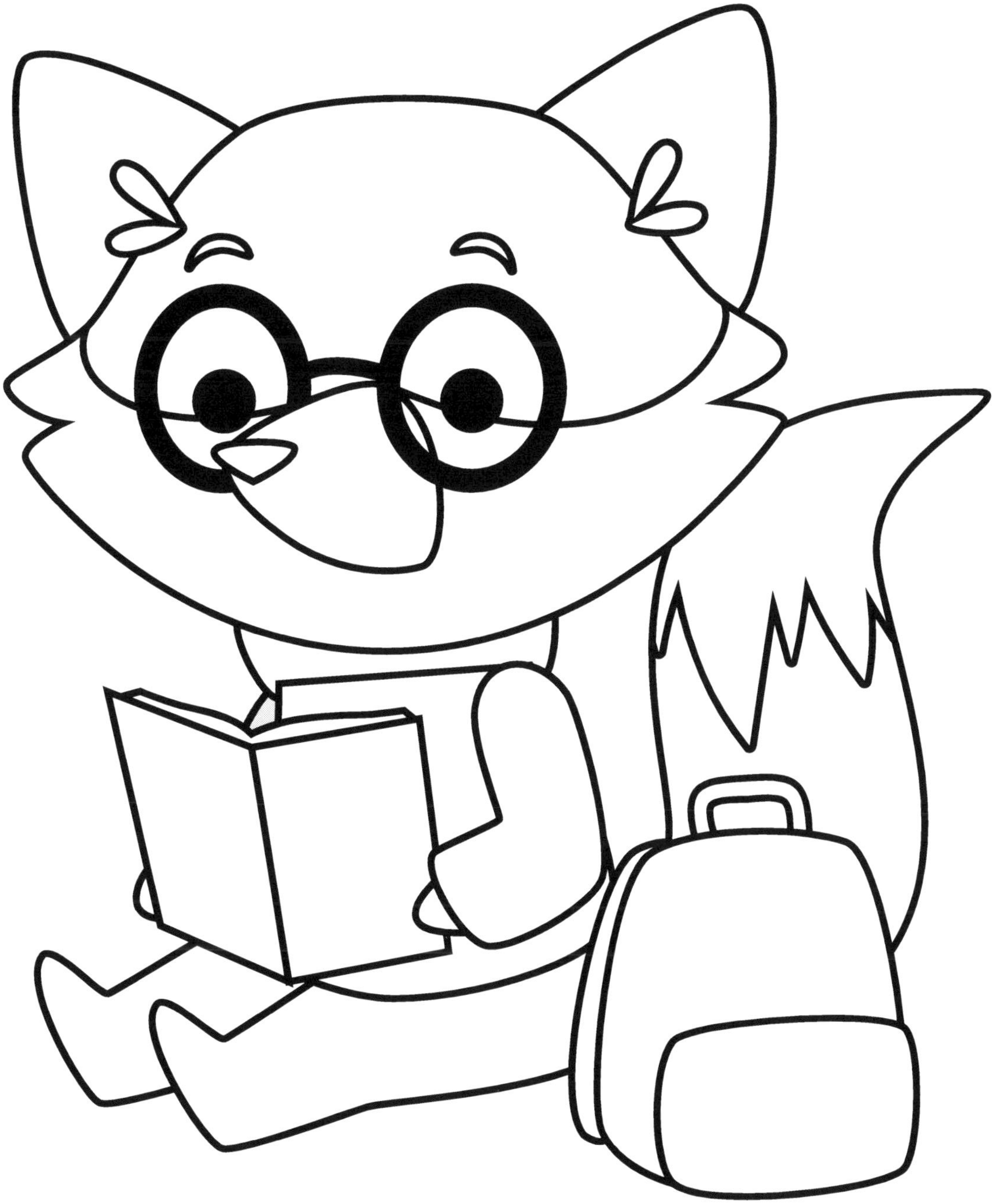

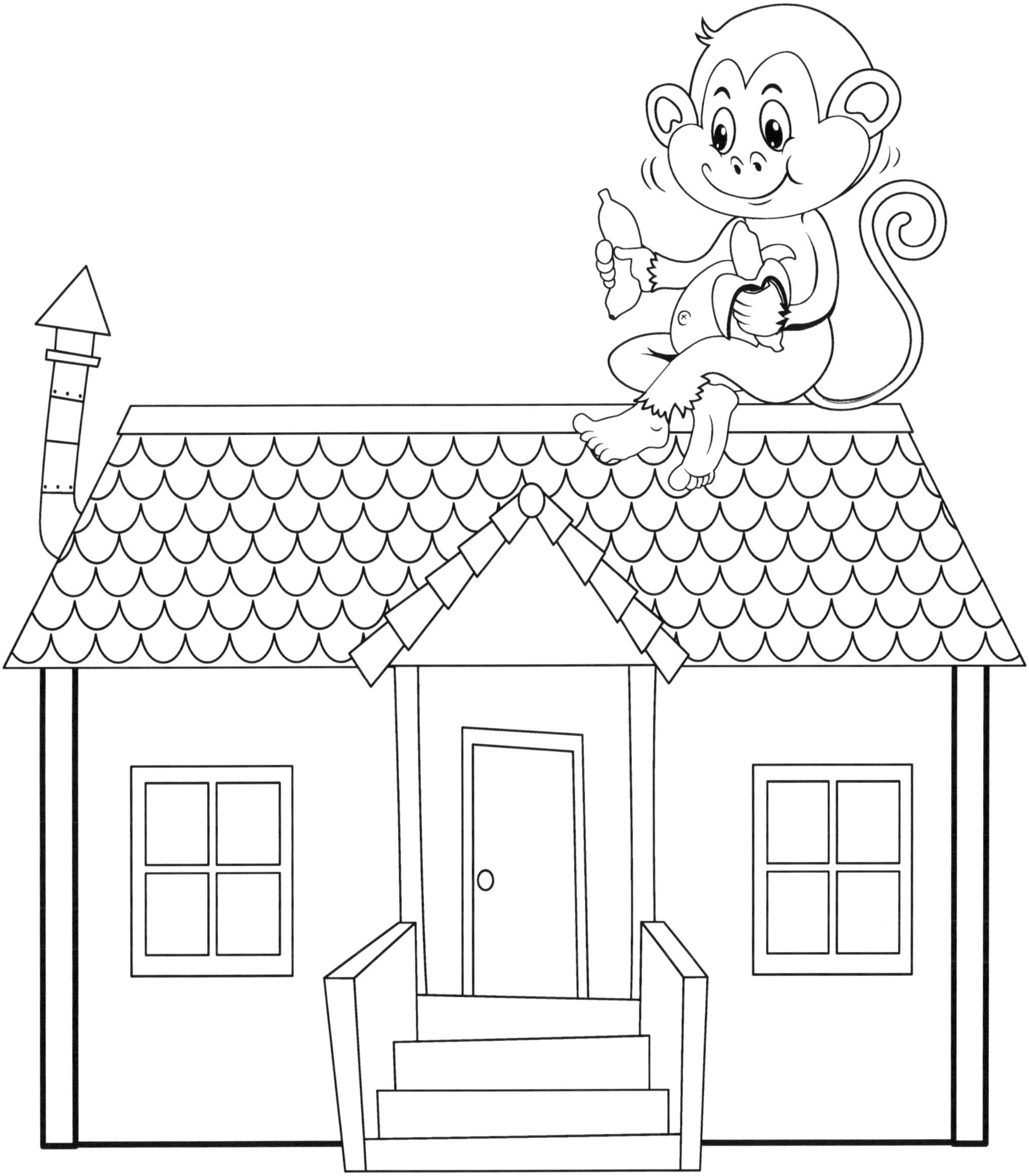

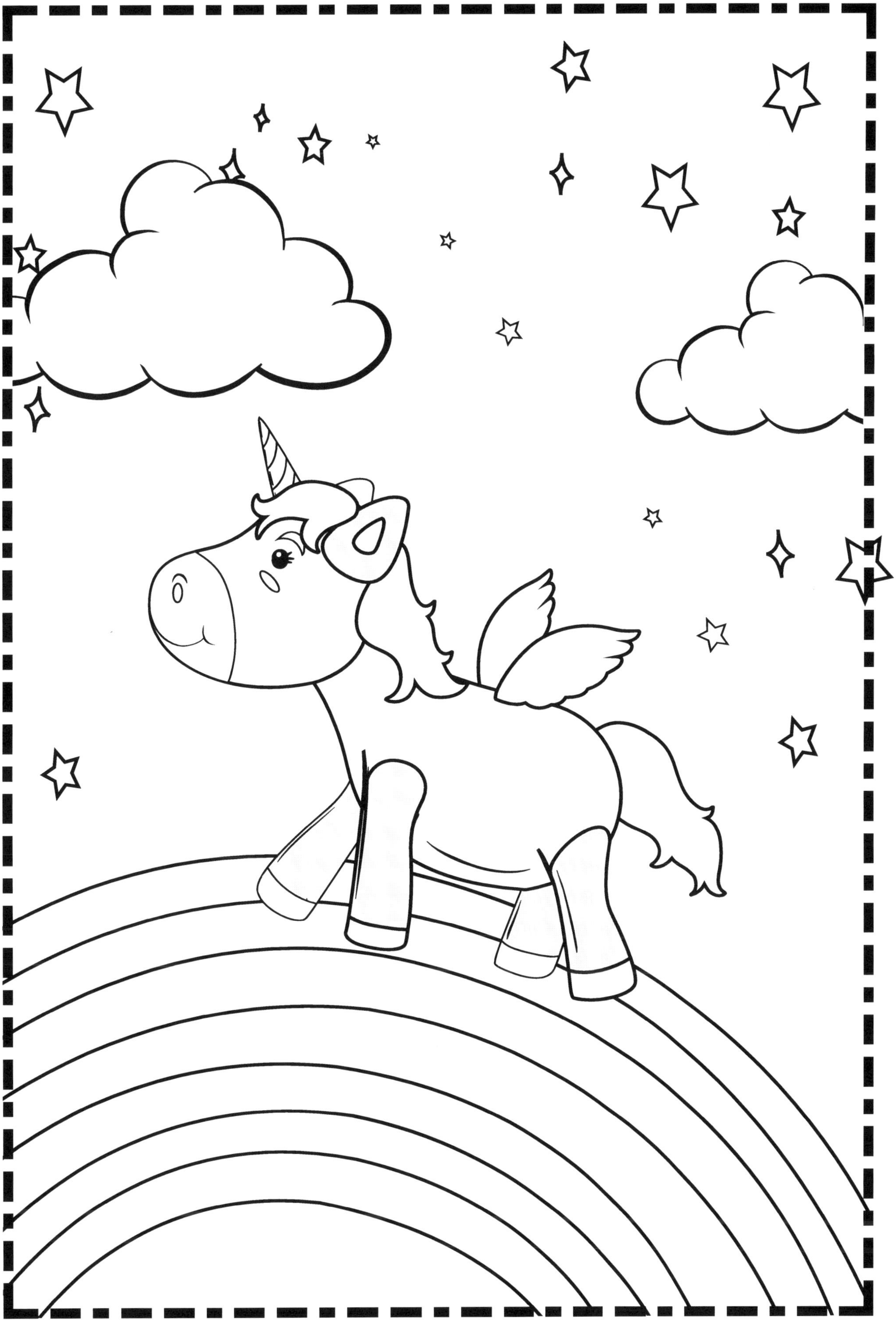

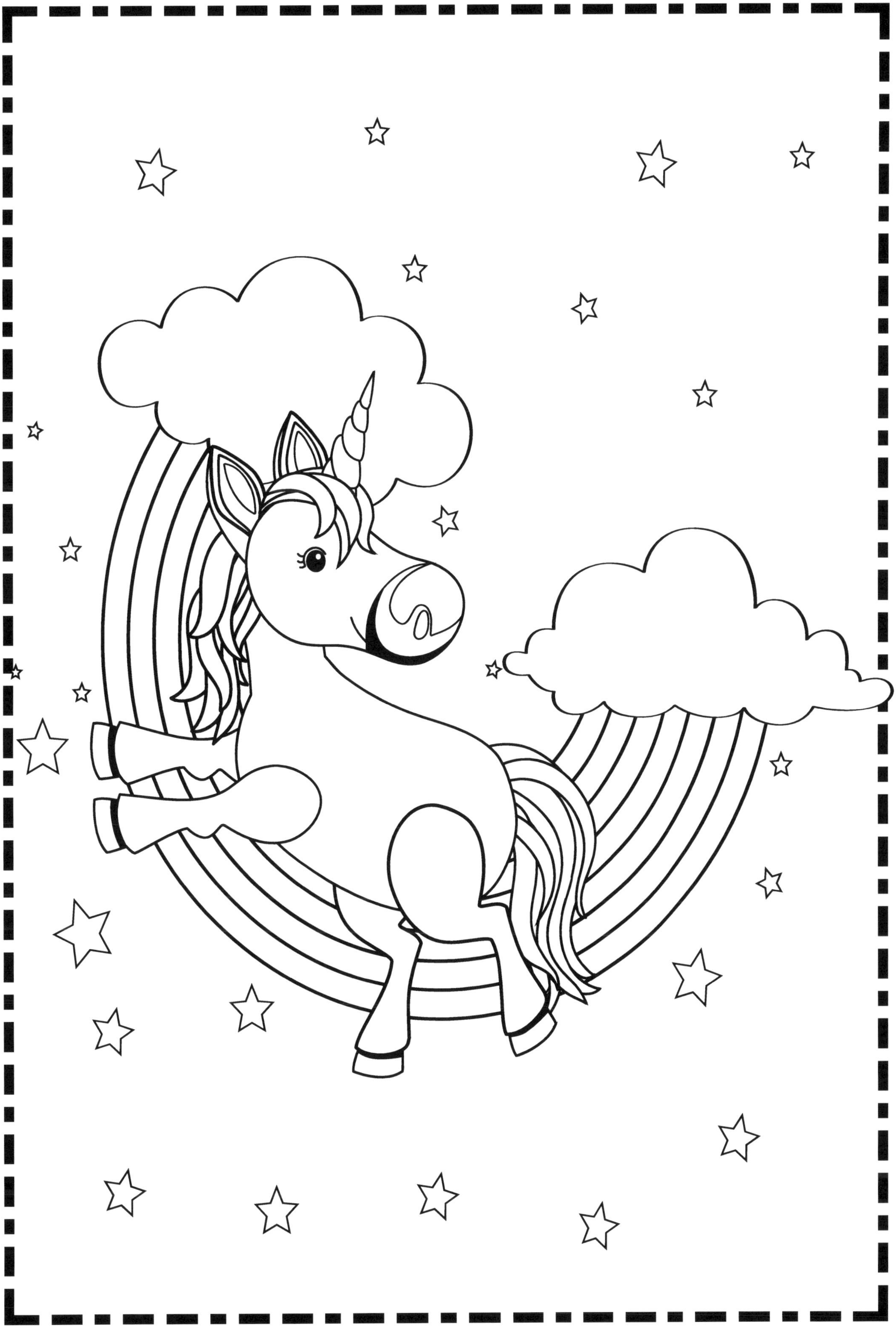

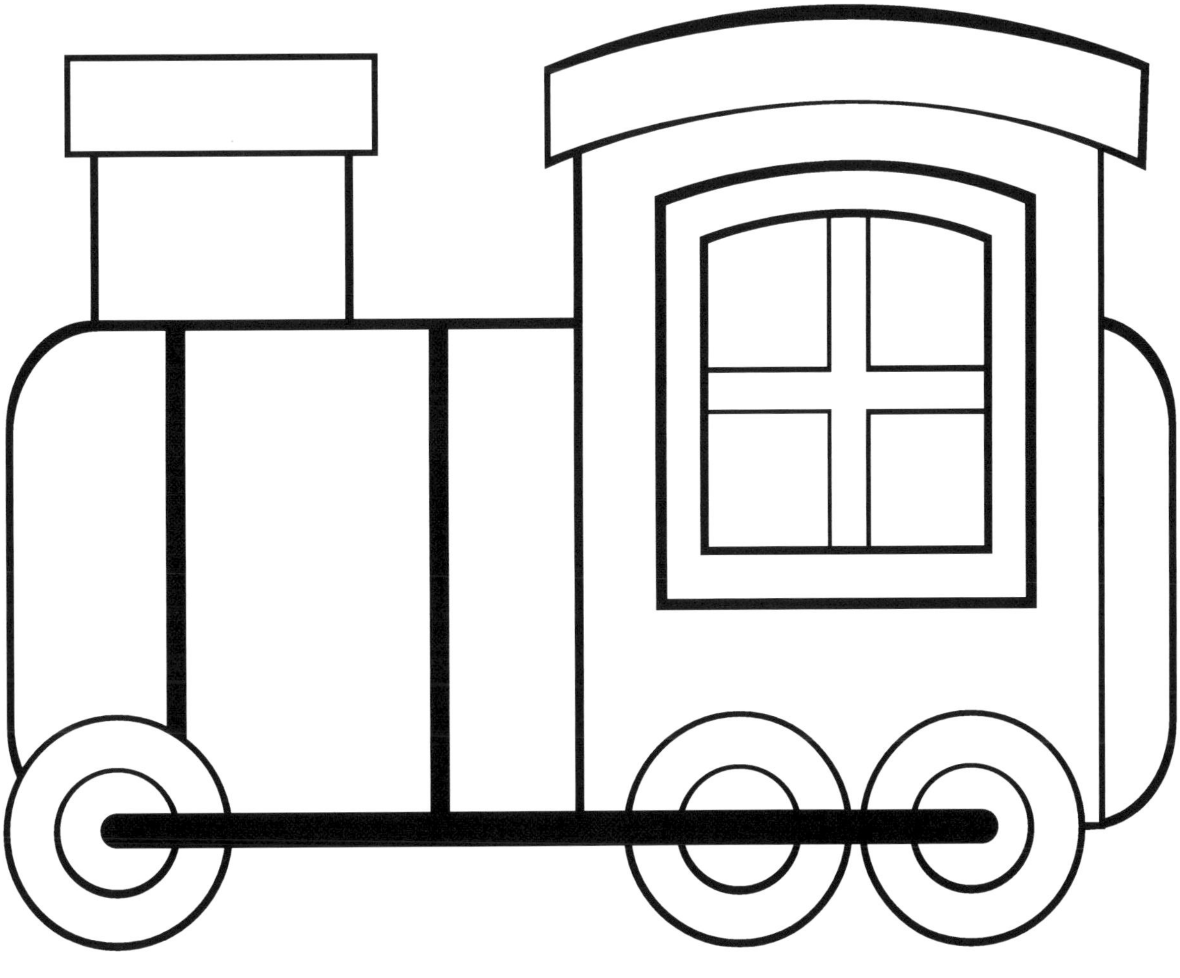

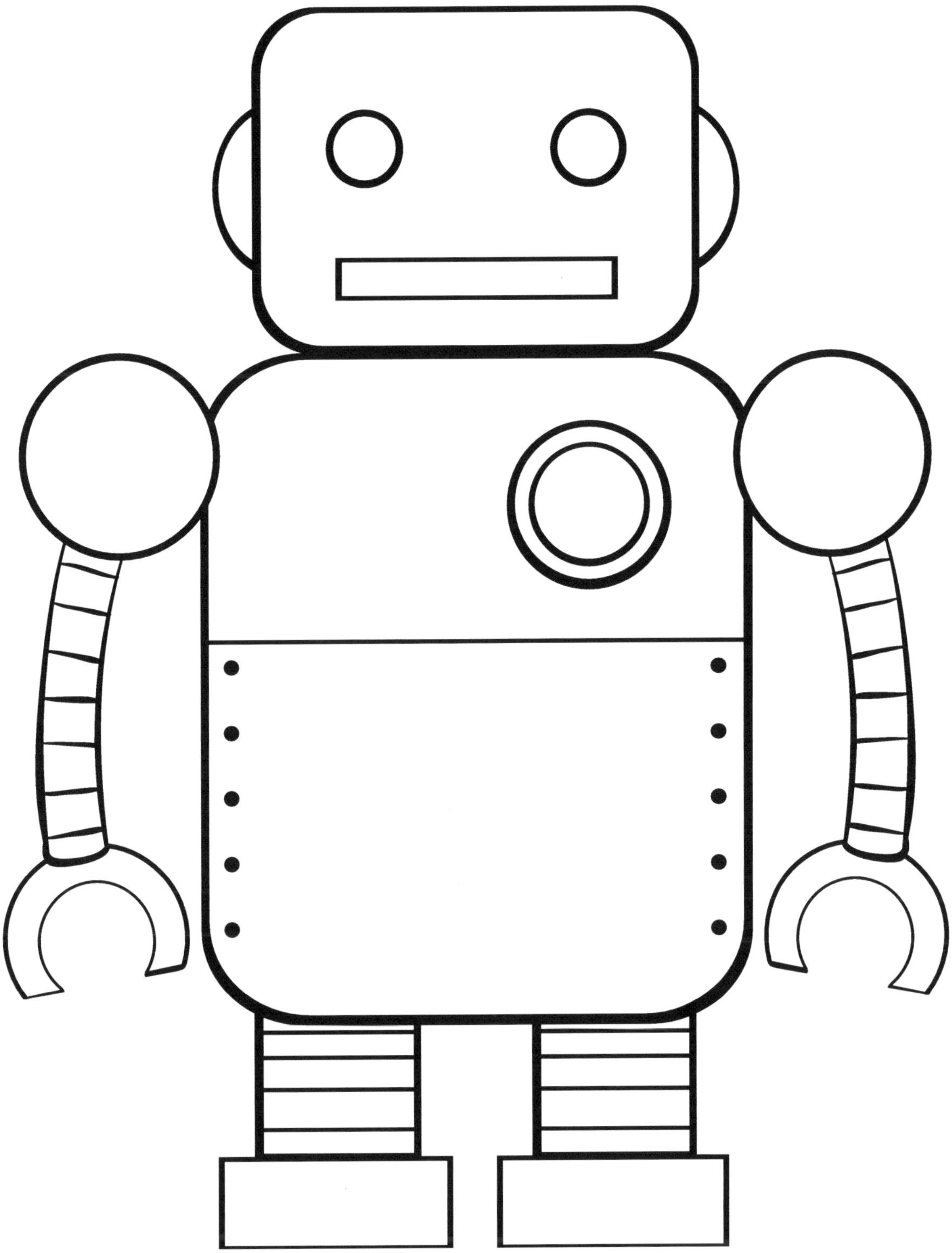

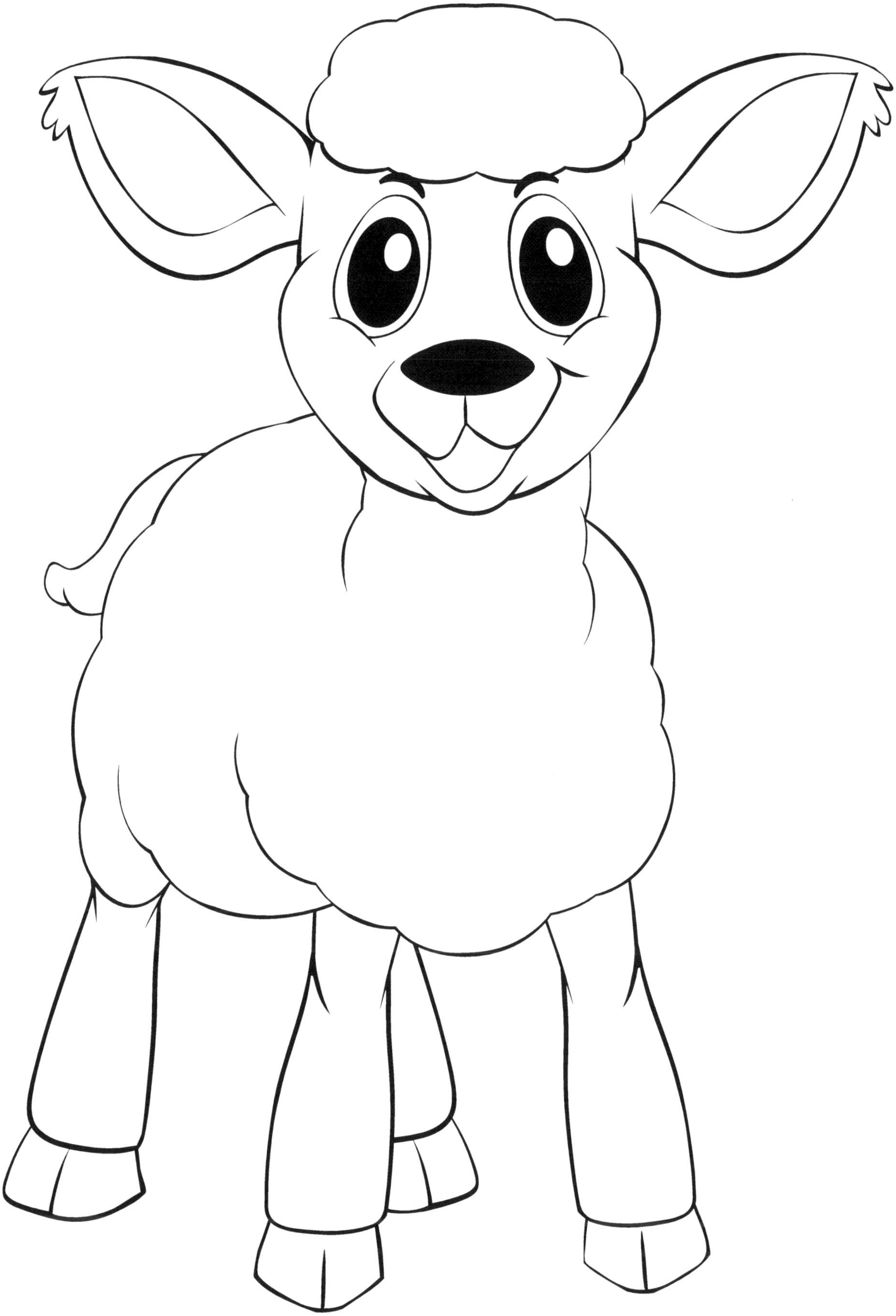

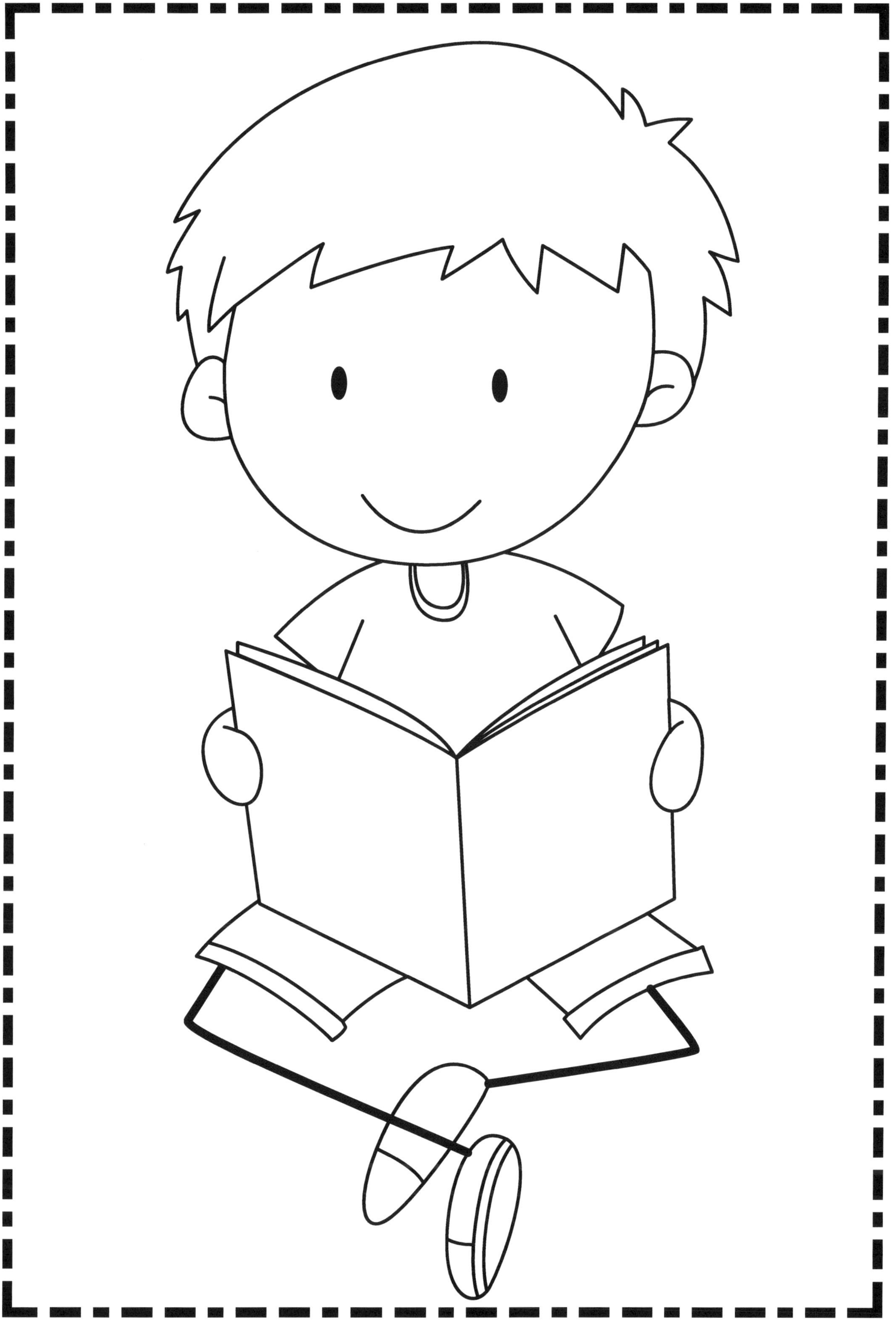

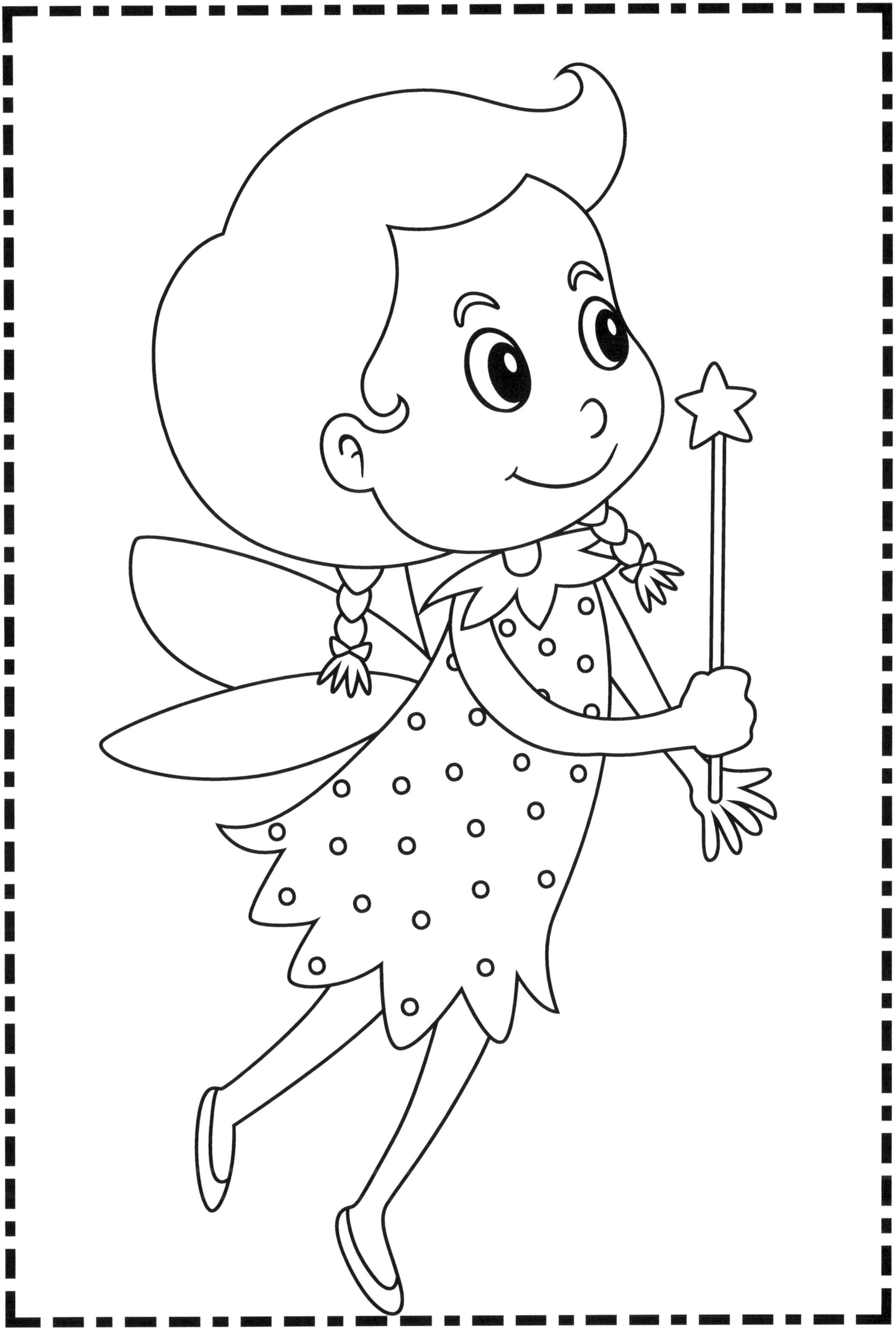

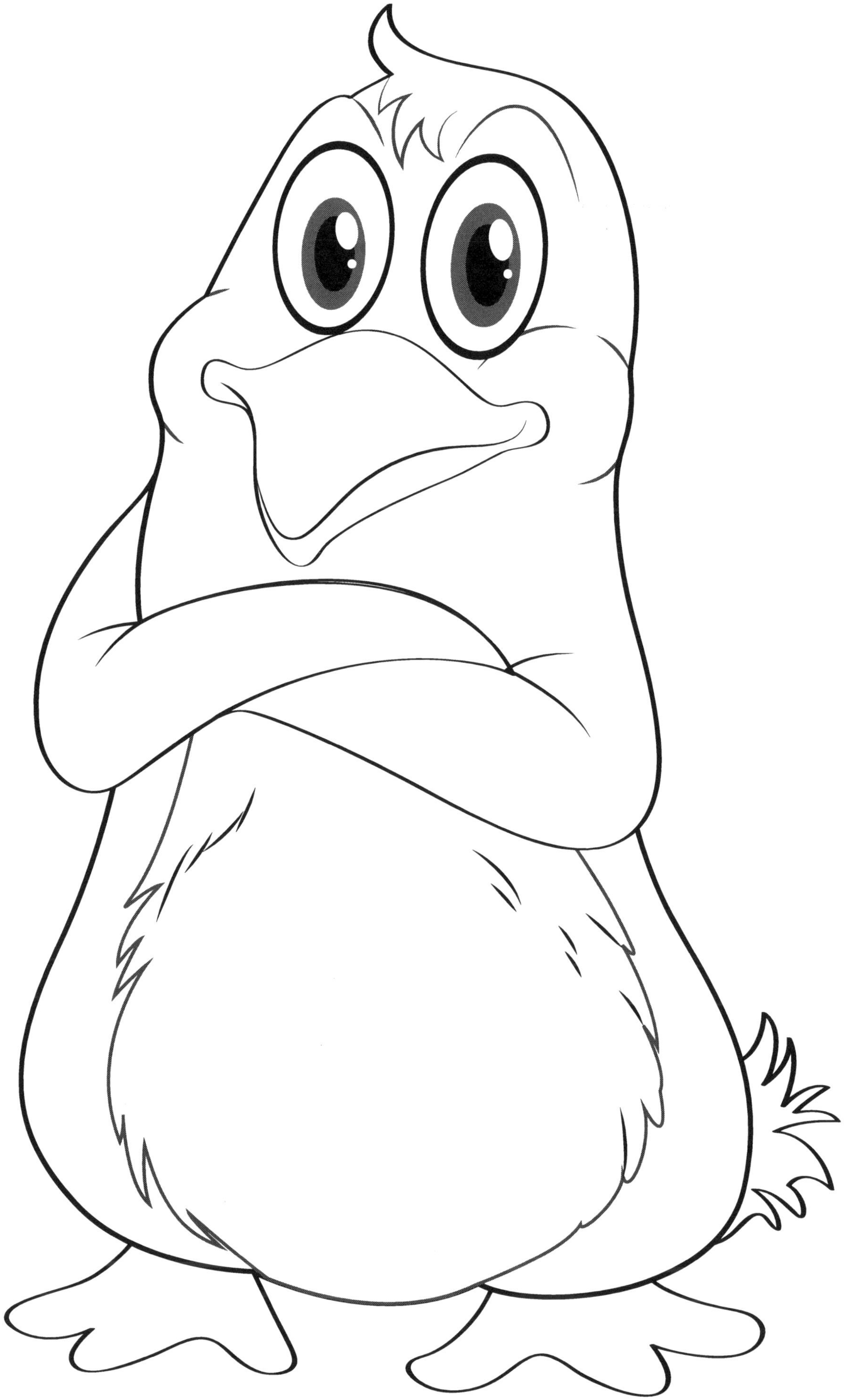

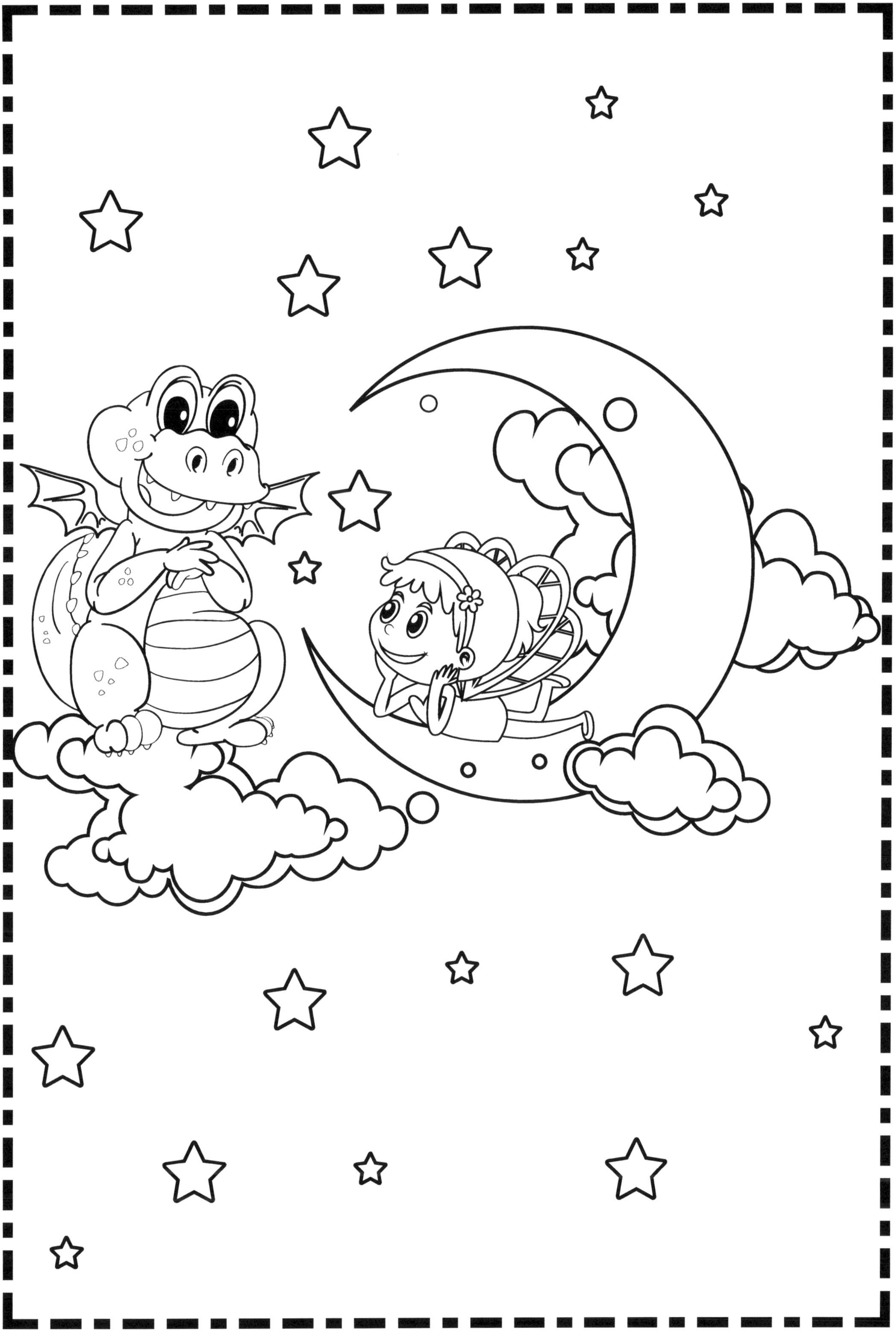

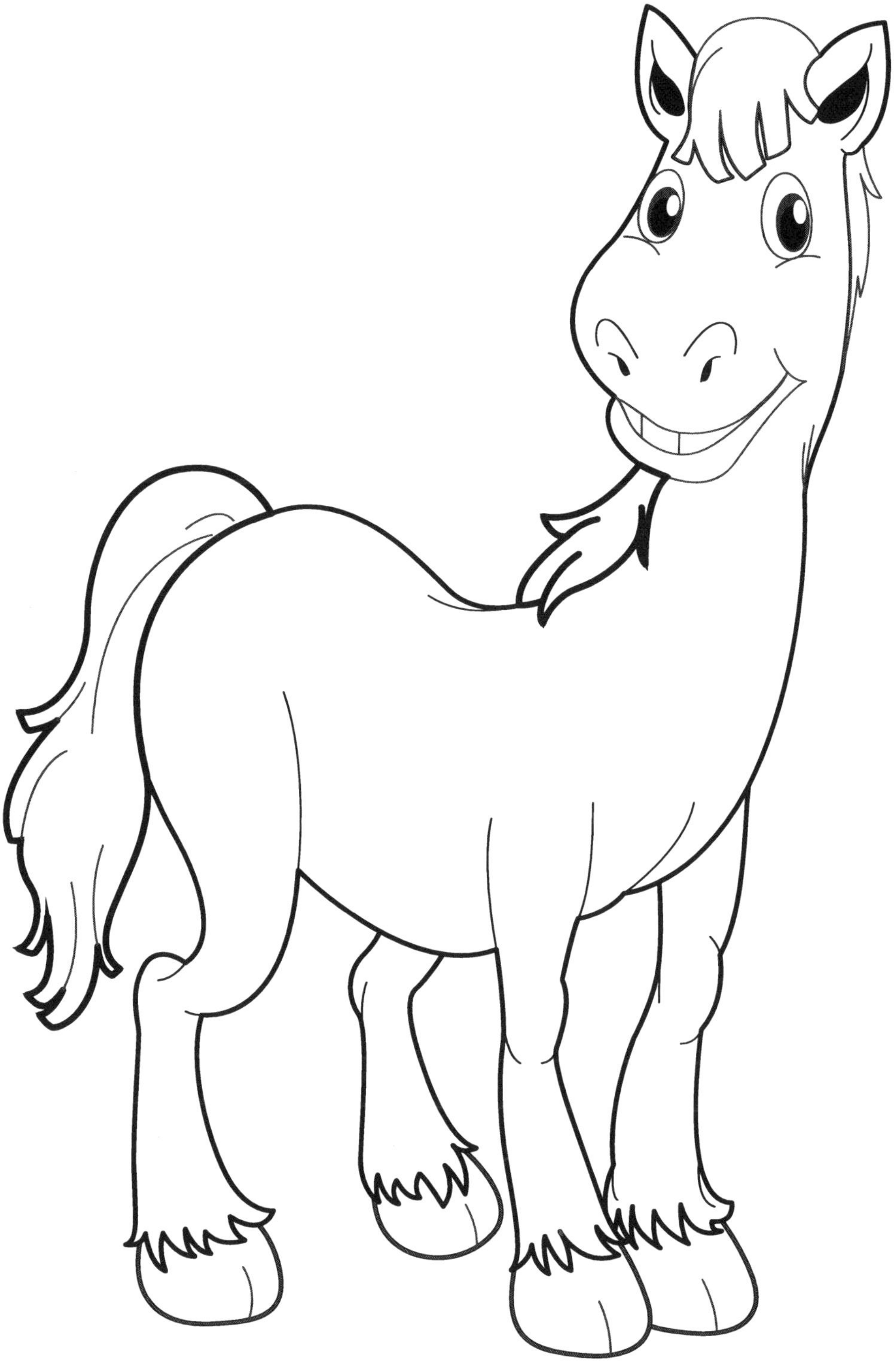

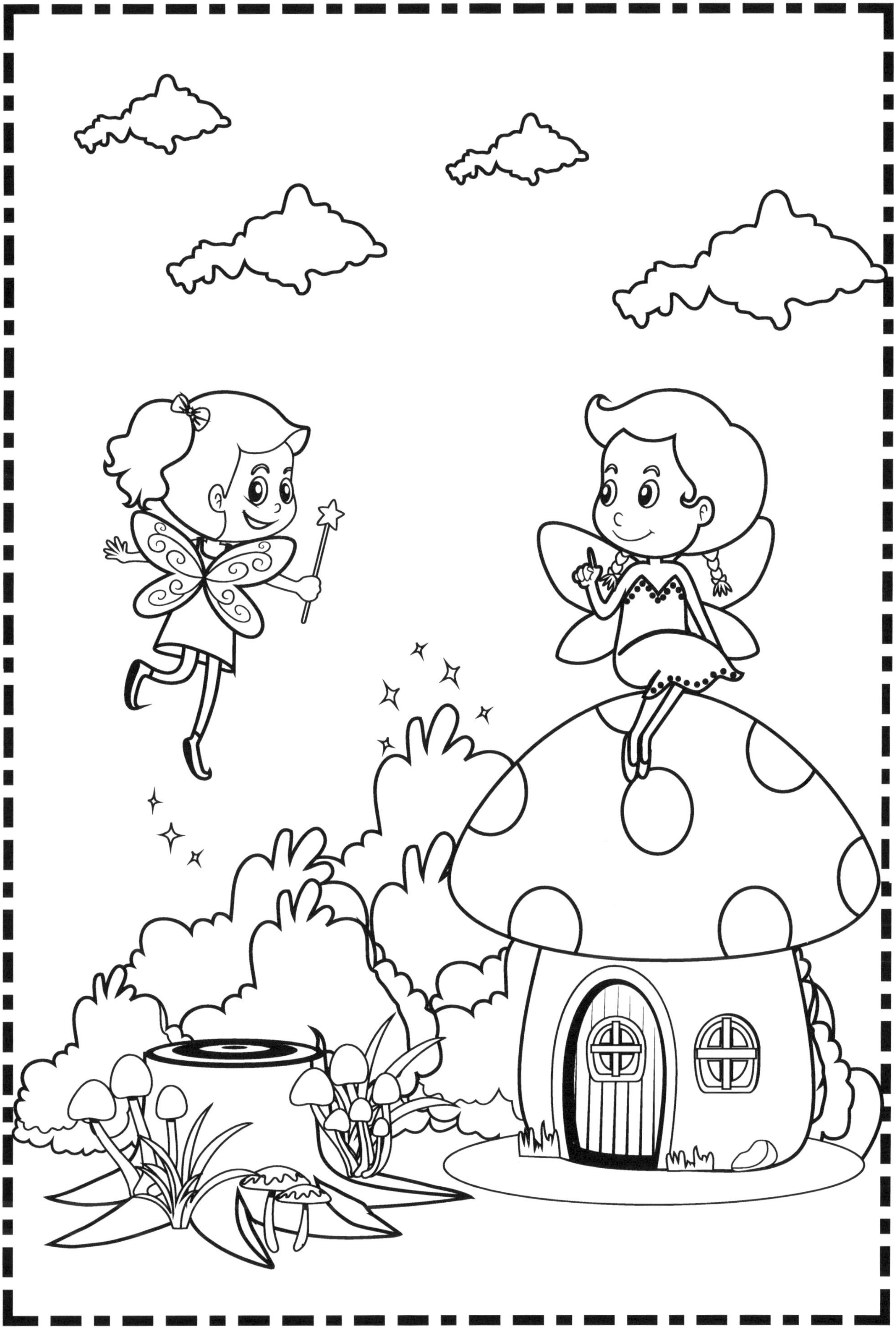

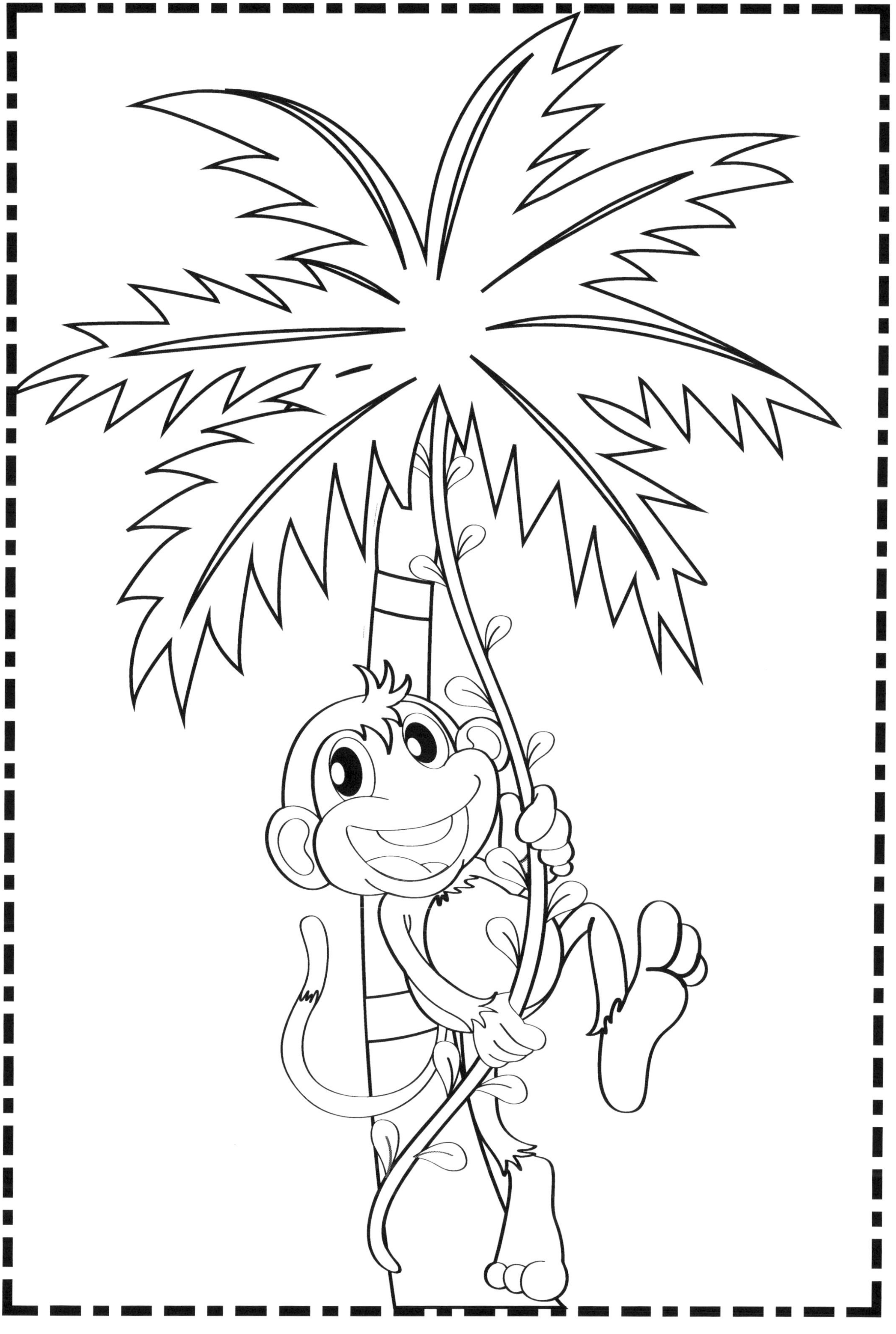

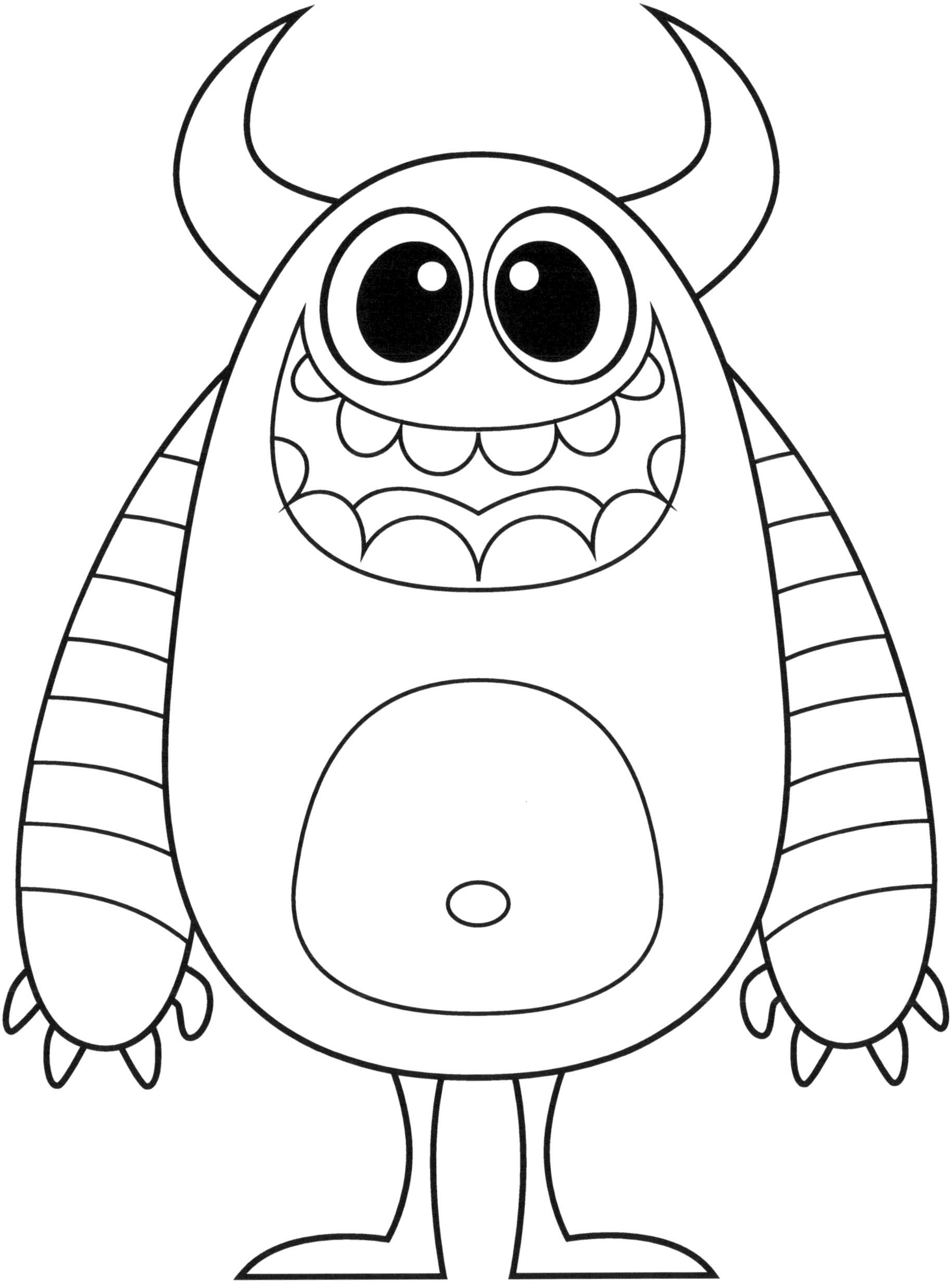

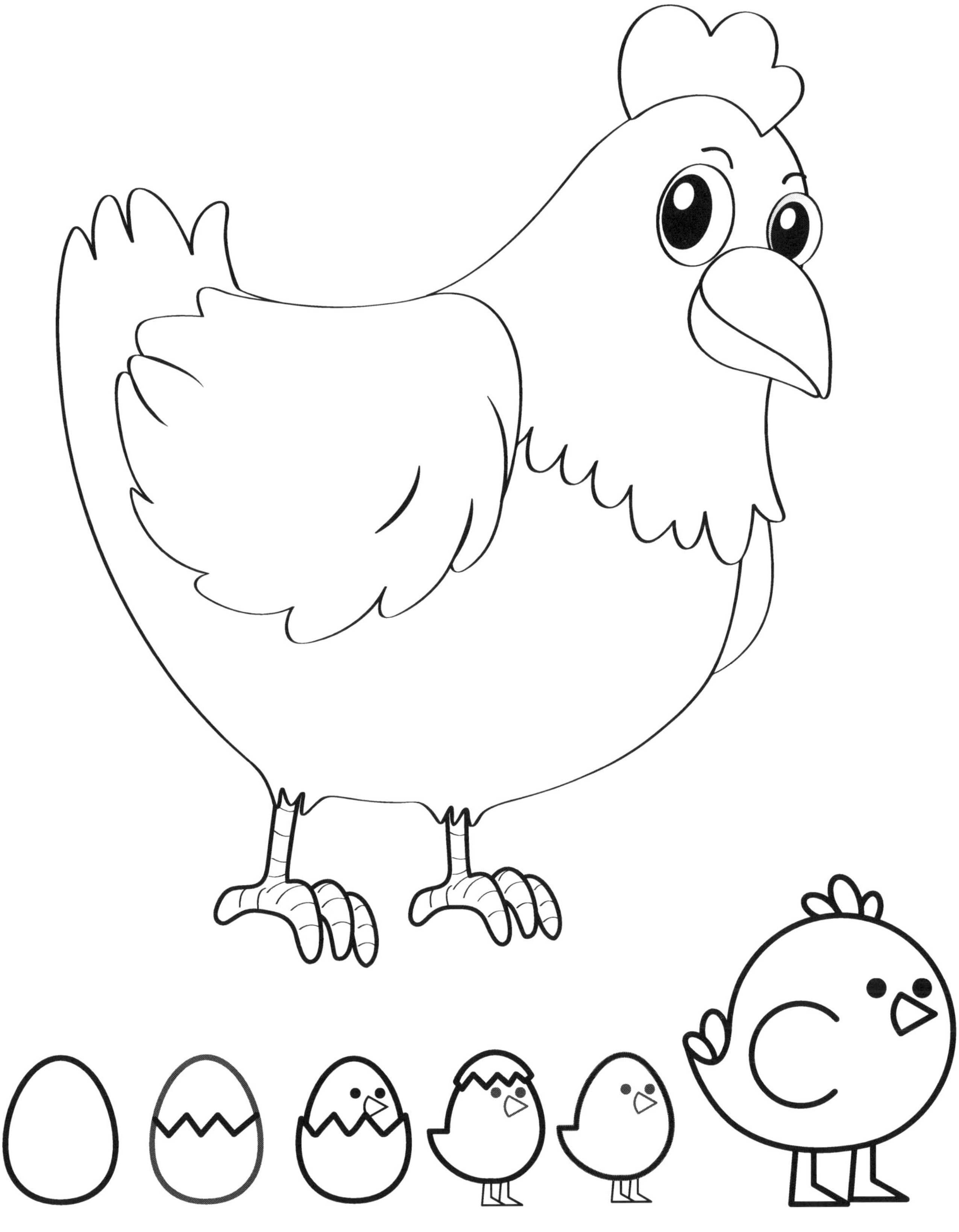

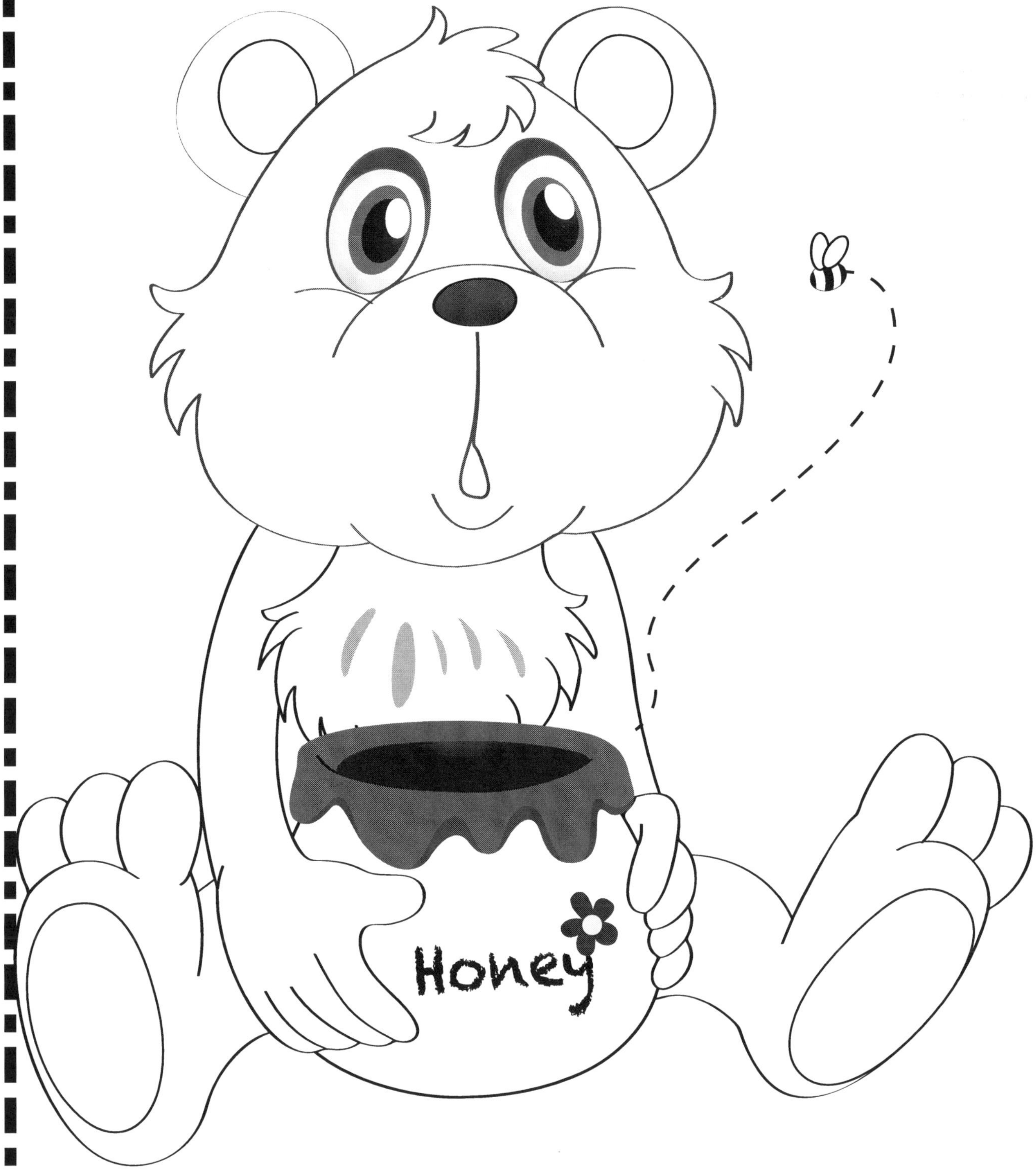
Honey

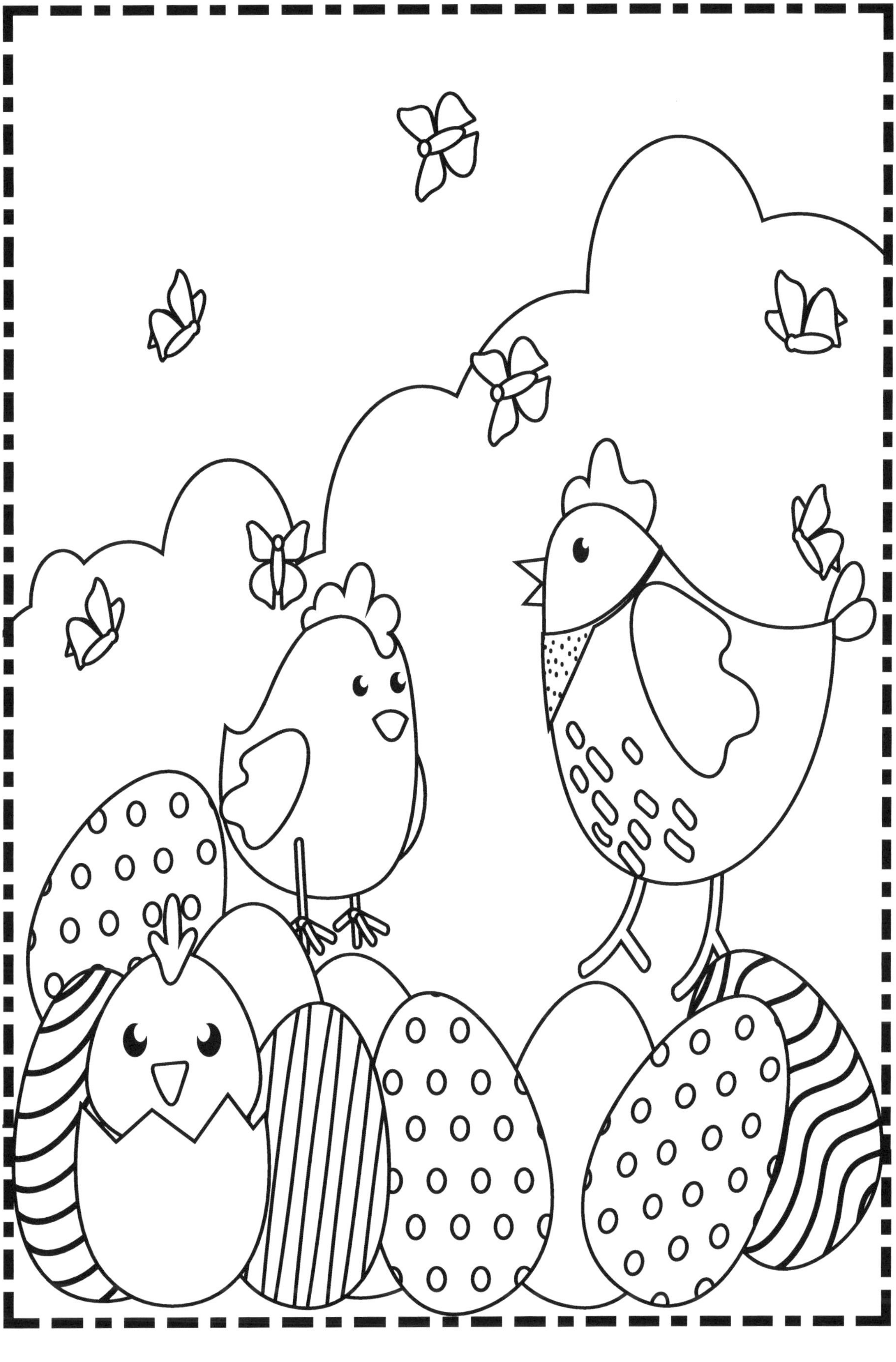

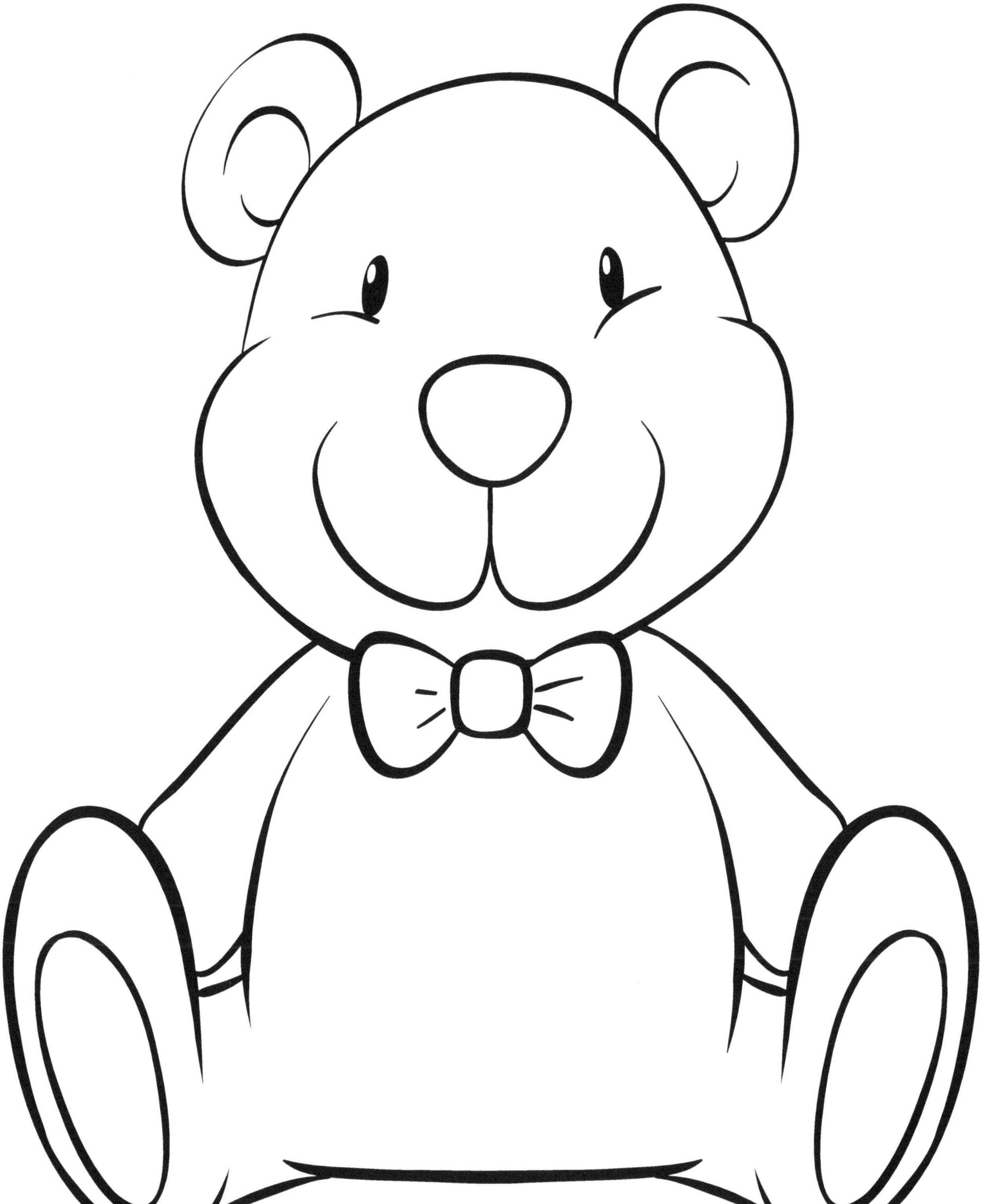

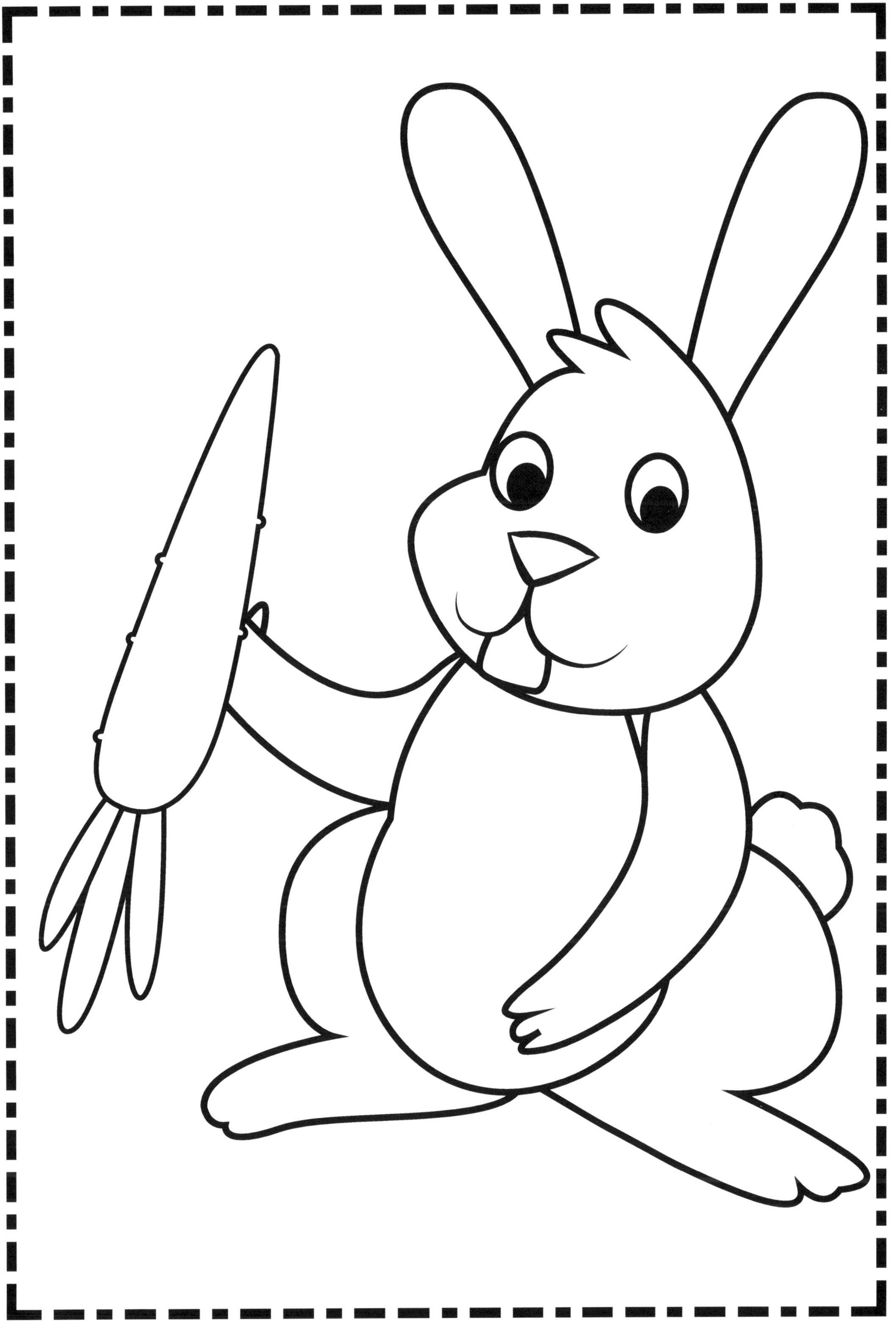